C -
975.4
Jy

D1529071

DATE DUE

1998	

PRINTED IN U.S.A.

The United States

West Virginia

Paul Joseph
ABDO & Daughters

visit us at
www.abdopub.com

Published by Abdo & Daughters, 4940 Viking Drive, Suite 622, Edina, Minnesota 55435.
Copyright © 1998 by Abdo Consulting Group, Inc., Pentagon Tower, P.O. Box 36036,
Minneapolis, Minnesota 55435 USA. International copyrights reserved in all countries.
No part of this book may be reproduced in any form without written permission from the
publisher.

Printed in the United States.

Cover and Interior Photo credits: Peter Arnold, Inc., SuperStock, Archive, Corbis-
Bettmann

Edited by Lori Kinstad Pupeza
Contributing editor Brooke Henderson
Special thanks to our Checkerboard Kids—Raymond Sherman, Annie O'Leary,
Matthew Nichols

All statistics taken from the 1990 census; The Rand McNally Discovery Atlas of The
United States.

Library of Congress Cataloging-in-Publication Data

Joseph, Paul, 1970-
    West Virginia / by Paul Joseph.
    p. cm. -- (United States)
    Includes index.
    Summary: A brief introduction to the geography, history, natural resources,
    industries, cities, and people of West Virginia.
    ISBN 1-56239-894-6
    1. West Virginia--Juvenile literature. [1. West Virginia.] I. Title. II. Series:
    United States (series)
    F241.3.J69   1998
    975.4--dc21
                                           97-35959
                                         CIP
                                         AC

Contents

Welcome to West Virginia

All of West Virginia lies in the Appalachian Highlands of the eastern United States. West Virginia is shaped roughly like an oval. It has two panhandles. One extends north and the other extends east.

There was no such place as West Virginia until the **American Civil War**. The area was known as the western part of Virginia.

The people that lived in the west wanted to stay loyal to the Union. The people from the east wanted to leave the Union. So the people from the west started their own state and named it West Virginia.

In land size, West Virginia is one of the smallest states in the country. Its land is very rugged and beautiful. Most of the state is mountainous. In fact, West Virginia is nicknamed the Mountain State. It also has many thick forests, wonderful lakes and rivers, and scenic valleys.

West Virginia's beautiful land and state parks have attracted **tourists** for many years. The first president of the United States, George Washington, spent a lot of time in West Virginia. Today, people enjoy the state for its **mineral** springs, hunting, skiing, rafting, and fishing.

West Virginia has many mountains.

Fun Facts

WEST VIRGINIA
Capital and Largest city
Charleston (57,287 people)
Area
24,124 square miles
(62,481 sq km)
Population
1,801,625 people
Rank: 34th
Statehood
June 20, 1863
(35th state admitted)
Principal river
Ohio River
Highest point
Spruce Knob;
4,862 feet (1,482 m)
Motto
Montani semper liberi
(Mountaineers are always free)
Song
"The West Virginia Hills" and
two others
Famous People
Pearl Buck, Thomas "Stonewall"
Jackson, Anna Jarvis

*S*tate Flag

*R*hododendron

*C*ardinal

*S*ugar Maple

About West Virginia

The Mountain State

Detail area

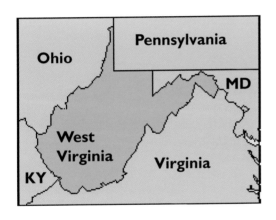

WV
West Virginia's
abbreviation

Borders: west (Ohio, Kentucky), north (Ohio, Pennsylvania), east (Maryland, Virginia), south (Virginia)

Nature's Treasures

The beautiful state of West Virginia has many treasures in its state. There are large scenic mountains, thick forests, pretty valleys, wonderful lakes and rivers, and rich **minerals**.

West Virginia is known as the Mountain State. Most of the mountains are covered in forests. Most of West Virginia is covered with forests. People from all around the world come to see all the wonderful mountain parks in the state.

The scenic valleys and canyons also attract visitors. Clear lakes and rivers ramble through state parks. People go white water rafting, fishing, and boating.

West Virginia's most valuable natural resources are the minerals found in the ground. Coal can be found in almost every part of West Virginia. Each year the state is one of the biggest producers of coal in the country.

Other treasures found under the ground are natural gas, stone, **petroleum**, sand, and gravel.

Springtime in West Virginia.

Beginnings

In 1669, **Governor** Berkeley of Virginia sent John Lederer to the western part of Virginia to **explore** the area. This mountainous region was mainly a hunting ground for **Native Americans**.

It wasn't until 1727 when people began settling in what is now West Virginia. Morgan Morgan built the first permanent home there. By 1775, about 30,000 people lived in this area.

In 1788, Virginia became the 10th state in the United States. The area now called West Virginia was also part of Virginia. For the next 70 years, the western part of Virginia grew away from the rest of the state. Separated by a mountain, the two sections became different in many ways.

The people from the east had slaves and wanted to

continue to have slaves. The people from the west didn't use slaves. Also the people from the east had more power when it came to state **government** and taxes.

Abolitionists were people who wanted slavery to end. Abolitionist John Brown formed a group of people to fight slavery. General Lee of the South stormed the armory where the abolitionists were meeting. Several people were killed. This was one of the battles that started the Civil War.

On June 20, 1863, the people in the western part of Virginia broke completely away from Virginia and became their own state.
The 35th state of the United States was named West Virginia.

John Brown's Fort in Harpers Ferry, West Virginia.

B.C. to 1726

Early Land and Settlers

 During the Ice Age, many thousands of years ago, West Virginia was covered by ice and glaciers. Many years later the ice began to melt and the mountains, valleys, and rivers began to form.

 1669: **Governor** Berkeley of Virginia sends John Lederer to **explore** what is now West Virginia.

 1726: Morgan Morgan settles near Bunker Hill.

West Virginia

B.C. to 1726

1742 to 1831

Discoveries and Differences

 1742: Coal is discovered on Coal River at Racine.

 1788: Virginia becomes a state. What is now West Virginia also becomes a state as part of Virginia.

 1815: The first gas well in the United States is drilled near Charleston.

 1831: The people from the eastern part of Virginia and the western part of Virginia fight about slavery. They separate themselves.

West Virginia

1742 to 1831

1863 to Present

Statehood and Beyond
1859: Abolitionist John Brown raids an armory in Harpers Ferry.

1863: West Virginia becomes their own state on June 20.

1907: Five mine disasters kill 537 people. One mine explosion alone killed 361 people.

1952: Bluestone Dam on the New River is completed.

1988: A Major oil spill pollutes the Monongahela and Ohio rivers. It endangers the water supply all the way from Pittsburgh, Pennsylvania, to Wheeling, West Virginia.

West Virginia

1863 to Present

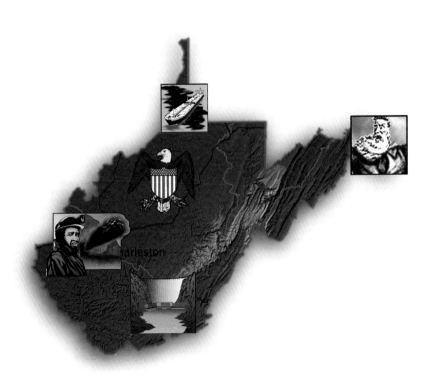

West Virginia's People

There are about 1.8 million people living in the state of West Virginia. It is the 34th largest state. The first known people to live on the land that is now West Virginia were **Native Americans**. They used the land as hunting grounds.

Many well-known people have come from West Virginia. Martin R. Delaney was born in Charles Town, Virginia, (now in West Virginia). He was an author, a physician, and a Civil Rights leader. Delaney was the first African-American field officer given a high rank in American history. He was made a major in the **American Civil War**.

Anna M. Jarvis was born in Grafton, West Virginia. She was the founder of Mother's Day. Following the death of her mother in 1907, Jarvis campaigned to have one day a year dedicated to mothers. In 1915, President Woodrow Wilson named the second Sunday of every May as Mother's Day.

Mary Lou Retton was born in Fairmont, West Virginia. She gained her fame as a gymnast. The tiny talent won four medals in the 1984 Olympics including a gold in the all-around competition.

Anna M. Jarvis

Mary Lou Retton

Martin R. Delaney

Splendid Cities

West Virginia has many splendid cities in its state with places to see and things to do. However, West Virginia doesn't have many large cities. Not one city in the state has even 100,000 people.

Most of the chief cities in the Mountain State are located in the river valleys. Charleston, the capital, is the largest city with just under 60,000 people. Charleston is an **industrial** city with many **manufacturing** jobs. It is also home to the Sunrise Art Museum and the University of Charleston college.

Huntington is the second largest city with just over 50,000 people. It is a port city on the Ohio River. Places

Wheeling

Clarksburg

Huntington

Charleston

20

of interest in Huntington are Ritter Park, Huntington Galleries, and Marshall University.

The third largest city is Wheeling with about 35,000 people. Fun things to do in Wheeling include visiting Oglebay Park and Wheeling Park. Jamboree USA and the Festival of Lights also take place in Wheeling.

Some of the other splendid cities in West Virginia are Morgantown, Fairmont, Beckley, Clarksburg, and Martinsburg.

The State Capitol Building in Charleston, West Virginia.

West Virginia's Land

West Virginia has some of the most beautiful land in the country. Most of the state is forested mountains. It also has narrow valleys, mixed in with clear lakes and rivers. This scenic state is divided into two natural regions.

The Valley and Ridge region covers most of the eastern panhandle and a narrow strip along the eastern and southern borders of the state. This area has both the lowest and highest points in the state. The lowest point is in the panhandle along

Allegheny Plateau

Valley and Ridge Region

the Potomac River. Only 100 miles to the southeast is Spruce Knob. That is the highest point in the state of West Virginia.

The other region is the Allegheny Plateau. It covers a very large part of the state. Along its eastern edge lies the Allegheny Mountains. To the west many streams have cut the land into a series of rounded hills.

West Virginia's biggest rivers are in this area. They drain into the Ohio River. These rivers are the Little Kanawha, Kanawha, Guyandotte, and Big Sandy.

West Virginia's Valley and Ridge Region.

West Virginia at Play

The people of West Virginia and the many people who visit the Mountain State have a lot of things to do and see.

Many **tourists** visit West Virginia's mountain **resorts**. The state's **mineral** springs have attracted visitors since the days of George Washington.

West Virginia's state parks attract more than a million visitors a year. The larger cities have their own fine parks such as Wheeling's Oglebay Park and Charleston's Coonskin Park.

The biggest recreational sport in the Mountain State is white water rafting. There are seven major rivers where people like to go rafting. One of the best places to raft is on the Gauley River.

Other fun things to do in West Virginia include skiing on the awesome mountains, hunting in the wonderful forests, and hiking in the scenic parks. People also enjoy fishing. The state has several rivers and lakes that are stocked with freshwater fish.

White water rafting is West Virginia's biggest recreational sport.

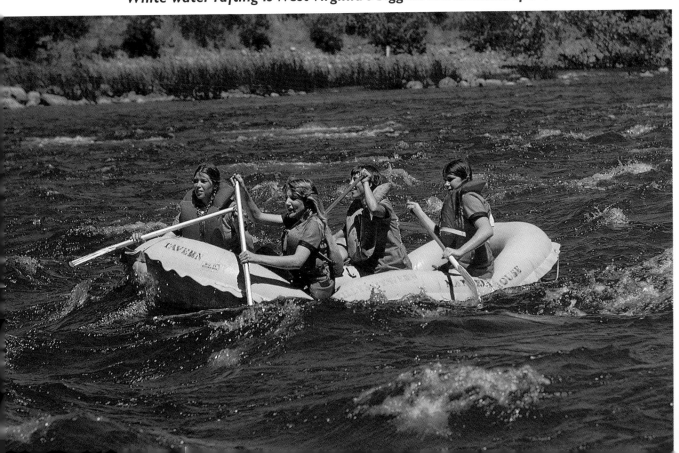

West Virginia at Work

The people of West Virginia must work to make money. Coal mining at one point was the state's leading **industry**. Today, it is **manufacturing**. Many of the people in the Mountain State work in some form of manufacturing.

West Virginia's manufacturing industries make more money than **mining**, farming, and forestry combined. Many people work in the huge chemical plants that are in the Kanawha Valley. Other people in the state make things out of metal.

Some people in West Virginia work as miners. Mining is still one of the leading industries in the state.

Many people work in service jobs because of the many visitors to the state. Service is working in hotels, **resorts**, restaurants, banks, and stores to name a few.

West Virginia offers many different things to do and see. Because of its natural beauty, people, mountains, forest, rivers, and cities, the Mountain State is a great place to visit, live, work, and play.

F&M coal strip mine in West Virginia.

Fun Facts

• West Virginia had a hard time choosing between two cities for the capital. In 1863, when West Virginia became a state, Wheeling was the capital. In 1870, the capital was moved to Charleston. In 1875, it was moved back to Wheeling. In 1885, it was moved back to Charleston, where it still is today.

• The name Virginia comes from Queen Elizabeth I of England. Because the area that is now West Virginia was part of Virginia at one point, the state decided to keep the name Virginia and put West in front of it.

• The state of West Virginia is nicknamed the Mountain State because the land is mostly mountainous. The people of West Virginia are nicknamed Mountaineers. The state motto is "Mountaineers Are Always Free." This is talking about the freedom from Virginia.

•Most of the marbles sold in America come from factories in Parkersburg, West Virginia.

West Virginia is named after Queen Elizabeth I of England.

Glossary

American Civil War: a war between groups from the southern states and the northern states of the United States between 1861-1865.

Confederacy: a group that bands together for a common belief. In this case it is the 11 southern states that left the Union between 1860 and 1861.

Descendants: people who are related to others who lived a long time ago.

Explorers: people that are one of the first to discover and look over land.

Government: the people that work for the country, state, city, or county.

Governor: the highest elected official in the state.

Industrial: big businesses such as factories or manufacturing.

Manufacture: to make things by machine in a factory.

Minerals: things found in the earth, such as rock, diamonds, or coal.

Miners: people who work underground to get minerals.

Native Americans: the first people who were born in and occupied North America.

Petroleum: also known as oil. An oily liquid that is drilled from wells in the ground. It is used to make gasoline, fuel oils, and other products.

Population: the number of people living in a certain place.

Resort: a place to vacation that has fun things to do.

Settlers: people that move to a new land where no one has lived before and build a community.

Tourists: people who travel for pleasure.

Internet Sites

West Virginia Web
http://wvweb.com/
The West Virginia Web is the most comprehensive site about West Virginia. We are dedicated to providing our state the opportunity to share its people, businesses, and places with the world.

West Virginia Whitewater
http://wvweb.com/www/travel_recreation/whitewater/
whitewater2.html
Welcome to West Virginia Whitewater! Over 200 miles of West Virginia rivers are designated for commercial rafting. From easy (I) to nearly impossible (VI) West Virginia Whitewater awaits you.

These sites are subject to change. Go to your favorite search engine and type in West Virginia for more sites.

PASS IT ON

Tell Others Something Special About Your State

To educate readers around the country, pass on interesting tips, places to see, history, and little unknown facts about the state you live in. We want to hear from you!

To get posted ɔn ABDO & Daughters website, E-mail us at "mystate@abdopub.com"

Index